Martin Luther King Jr.

History Maker Bios

Mary Winget

LERNER PUBLICATIONS COMPANY • MINNEAPOLIS

This book is dedicated to my son, Bryan

Illustrations by Tim Parlin

Text copyright © 2003 by Lerner Publications Company
Illustrations copyright © 2003 by Lerner Publications Company

Lerner Publications Company
A division of Lerner Publishing Group
241 First Avenue North
Minneapolis, MN 55401 U.S.A.

Website address: www.lernerbooks.com

Library of Congress Cataloging-in-Publication Data

Winget, Mary.
    Martin Luther King Jr. / by Mary Winget.
        p.   cm. — (History maker bios)
    Summary: A biography focusing on the beliefs and accomplishments of civil rights leader Martin Luther King Jr.
    Includes bibliographical references (p. 47) and index.
    ISBN: 0-8225-4674-4 (alk. paper)
    1. King, Martin Luther, Jr., 1929-1968—Juvenile literature. 2. African Americans—Biography—Juvenile literature. 3. Civil rights workers—United States—Biography—Juvenile literature. 4. Baptists—United States—Clergy—Biography—Juvenile literature. 5. African Americans—Civil rights—History—20th century—Juvenile literature. [1. King, Martin Luther, Jr., 1929-1968. 2. Civil rights workers. 3. Clergy. 4. African Americans—Biography.] I. Title. II. Series.
    E185.97.K5W56 2003
    323'.092—dc21   2002010039

Manufactured in the United States of America
    2 3 4 5 6 – JR – 08 07 06 05 04 03

TABLE OF CONTENTS

INTRODUCTION

When Martin Luther King Jr. was born, black Americans did not have the same rights as white Americans. Since slavery times, black Americans had faced unfair treatment and sometimes violence. King dreamed of equality for all people, no matter what their skin color. He led a great struggle for the rights of black people. But he didn't use weapons. He used words and actions. He was jailed and beaten, but he never gave up. Because of King's peaceful words and work, black Americans—and all Americans—have more freedom.

This is his story.

1 LIFE'S LESSONS

Martin Luther King Jr. was born in Atlanta, Georgia, on January 15, 1929. He lived in a large house with his parents, his brother, his sister, and his grandparents.

One day, just like almost every day, Martin went across the street to play with his friend. He rang the doorbell.

His friend's mother came to the door. She didn't invite him in, as she usually did. Instead she told Martin that he couldn't play over there anymore.

Martin ran home to his mother, crying and wondering how this could be. Martin's mother held him in her arms. She tried to explain. He was black. His friend was white. Now that the boys would be starting school, his friend's mother did not want them to play together. It wasn't fair. But it was the way many white people felt.

Most of the time, black children could only play with other black children, as this photo of a birthday party shows. Martin is fourth from right.

Martin's mother told him that he was "as good as anyone." She told him not to think too much about what had happened. But it didn't make sense to Martin, and he never forgot the pain of that day.

Segregation, or separation, of races was the way it worked in Georgia—and all over the southern United States. Black children and white children went to separate schools. Black people and white people went to different churches. They couldn't even use the same drinking fountains. Signs everywhere reminded people: WHITES ONLY, BLACKS ONLY.

To eat at this southern restaurant, blacks and whites had to use separate entrances.

Businesses for black people, such as this store in Florida, were often in poor condition.

Segregation existed because many white people believed that black people did not deserve to live as well as white people lived. Some white people resented the rights African Americans had gained since slavery ended in 1865. They found all kinds of ways to keep black people down. The best jobs went to white people. Blacks were often kept from voting, and black schools had little money and few resources.

The King household included (BACK ROW) Martin's mother, father, and grandmother, and (FRONT ROW) Martin, his sister, Christine, and his brother, A.D.

Martin's father, called Daddy King, was a minister. Martin liked to listen to him preach on Sundays at Ebenezer Baptist Church. Daddy King's words could make people feel happy or sad. Martin learned that words were powerful. He especially liked big words.

Martin was a good student. He liked reading, and he enjoyed his speech class. Martin did well in speech contests. He got to use his own big words in speeches.

Martin began going to Morehouse College in Atlanta when he was only fifteen years old. Morehouse was a school for black men. Martin thought he wanted to study to be a doctor or a lawyer. But in his junior year, he decided to become a minister, like his father.

After he graduated from Morehouse, Martin went to school in the North. He went to Crozer Theological Seminary in Chester, Pennsylvania, to study religion.

Cool Guy

When Martin was a teenager, he liked to wear nice clothes, especially fashionable suits made of tweed. So his friends called him Tweed. Martin also enjoyed dancing. But Daddy King didn't approve. Dancing was against the rules of their church. After Martin was caught at a dance, he had to apologize to the whole church on a Sunday. That was hard to do. But it didn't make him stop dancing.

Gandhi lived from 1869 until 1948. He believed that all violence was wrong.

At Crozer, Martin learned about the life of Mohandas Gandhi. Gandhi lived in India when it was ruled by Great Britain. Many Indians suffered under unfair British laws. Gandhi wanted to change those laws, but only in peaceful ways. He taught the Indian people to fight for their rights without using violence. He organized worker protests and marches. This was called nonviolent resistance. It worked—finally, the British listened to the Indians' demands and gave them their freedom.

The idea of nonviolent resistance impressed Martin. It was hard for black people in the United States to stand up for their rights. Blacks who spoke out risked being beaten or killed. Martin wondered if black people in the United States could work together for peaceful change like the Indians had. Maybe they could use nonviolent resistance to win justice and equality.

Martin graduated from Crozer in 1951. He went to Boston University in Massachusetts to continue his ministry studies.

Martin lived in this building at Crozer, where he studied from 1948 until 1951.

In Boston, Martin met Coretta Scott. Coretta was from Alabama. She was studying to become a classical singer. At first Coretta thought Martin might be too stuffy. But once she got to know him, she thought he was charming. Martin admired Coretta's intelligence and beauty. The two fell in love. They were married on June 18, 1953.

After they both graduated, Martin and Coretta decided to move south. Martin took a job as a minister at Dexter Avenue Baptist Church in Montgomery, Alabama. Martin hoped he could help improve the lives of black people there.

2 LIFE IN MONTGOMERY

The people of Dexter Avenue Baptist Church welcomed Coretta and Martin to Montgomery. The young couple made many friends. Their family grew, too. On November 17, 1955, their daughter Yolanda was born.

Martin Luther King saw big changes happening for the whole United States, too. In 1954, the Supreme Court, the most important court in the country, had ruled that school segregation must end. Black children and white children had to be allowed to go to school together. Brave black people were standing up for their rights, and they were having some success.

BROWN VS. BOARD OF EDUCATION OF TOPEKA

Brown vs. Board of Education of Topeka was a historical Supreme Court decision. The Court ruled that segregation in public schools was wrong. Until this time, separate schools had been seen as equal schools. But black schools often had little money and were run-down. It was hard for children to learn there. The Supreme Court declared that this kind of segregation had to stop. After the decision, people began to wonder if other places—buses, trains, and rest rooms—could be desegregated, too.

Rosa Parks worked as a seamstress at a department store.

Rosa Parks was one such brave person. On December 1, 1955, she got on a bus after work. Montgomery's law said that black people had to sit in a section separate from white people. Rosa sat in the first row of the black section. Soon more white people got on, and the white section filled up. The bus driver ordered the people in Rosa's row to give up their seats. Rosa refused. The police came and arrested her.

The next day, King and another minister, Ralph Abernathy, learned about Rosa's arrest. The men decided to organize a bus boycott. Black people would refuse to ride the buses for one day.

On Monday morning, December 5, Martin and Coretta watched as the first buses went by their house. To their amazement, no black people were riding the buses. In fact, no black people rode the buses all day.

That afternoon, King and other black leaders met to decide what to do next. They formed the Montgomery Improvement Association (MIA) to continue the boycott until bus segregation in Montgomery ended.

Black riders on this Alabama bus stand, even though there are empty seats in the white section.

King encourages Montgomery's black community to stay off the buses.

Thousands of people packed into a meeting that night at the Holt Street Baptist Church. King told the crowd that it was time for them to demand equal rights. Peaceful—not violent—methods were the way to do it. "The only weapon that we have in our hands this evening is the weapon of protest," he said. King's powerful words inspired the audience. When he finished, they stood and cheered.

The next day, African Americans drove, got rides, or walked to work. They kept it up day after day. Such a large group of African Americans had never before stood together against segregation.

The white people of Montgomery were frightened by the boycott. Most of them didn't want black people to gain power. They thought King was a troublemaker. Angry white people sent death threats to King. They called him late at night telling him to leave Montgomery. King wondered if it would be safer for his wife and baby if the family did leave town. But a voice deep within told him to stay and stand up for justice and truth.

An empty bus rolls through downtown Montgomery during the bus boycott.

2843

"EASE THAT SQUEEZE"

RIDE THE BUS!

Black people formed car pools so that former bus riders could still get to work.

One night in January, while King was at a meeting, his house was bombed. King rushed home and made sure that Coretta and Yolanda had not been hurt. Outside, a crowd of black supporters had gathered. They were angry about the bombing. King calmed them down. He reminded them to act peacefully, even when others were violent toward them.

The bus boycott continued. Other houses were bombed. Some African Americans who walked to work were beaten. Many boycotters lost their jobs. Still, the black people of Montgomery peacefully kept up the boycott through the spring, the summer, and the following fall.

Finally, in December 1956, Montgomery's bus segregation law was changed. Bus segregation had to end. Martin Luther King and a white friend rode together in the front section of a city bus. The boycott had succeeded.

King (SECOND ROW, LEFT), along with Ralph Abernathy (FRONT LEFT), rides Montgomery's first desegregated bus on December 21, 1956.

3 LEADING THE STRUGGLE

Black people across the country were inspired by Martin Luther King and the boycotters in Montgomery. They started to come together to demand their civil rights—the right to life, freedom, and equal treatment. King continued speaking about working for civil rights without using violence.

MARTIN AND THE SCLC

Martin organized a meeting of sixty African American ministers from ten southern states in January 1957. Like Martin, the ministers wanted to work for civil rights using nonviolent resistance. They formed the Southern Christian Leadership Council (SCLC), and they chose Martin to be their president. Martin, the other ministers, and members of African American churches were united in working for civil rights all over the South.

In 1959, Martin and Coretta traveled to India. They saw where Mohandas Gandhi had worked, and they learned more about nonviolent resistance. Martin learned how Gandhi had gone to jail for breaking laws he thought were unfair. This method of nonviolent resistance brought attention to unfair laws. King decided he was willing to do this, too. King would peacefully break unjust laws and go to jail if he had to.

Back in the United States, King decided to devote all his time to civil rights. He left his job in Montgomery and moved back home to Atlanta.

Meanwhile, King's ideas were catching on. For example, black college students all over the South organized sit-ins. They sat at white-only lunch counters. No one would serve them. Often, white people yelled and threw food at the students. But the students never responded with violence.

Police lead these young black men away from a sit-in at a store in Nashville, Tennessee, in 1960.

King sits down to a rare dinner at home with Coretta and their children.

King was often away from home, speaking and organizing. But he tried to find time for his growing family. He and Coretta had three more children—Martin Luther III, Dexter, and Bernice. King liked playing with his children as well as reading to them in the evening.

Soon after Bernice was born in March 1963, King went to Birmingham, Alabama. Birmingham was one of the most segregated cities in the country. King wanted to help black people there win their civil rights. It was his biggest challenge yet.

King led peaceful marches. Thousands of black people came together on the streets of Birmingham. They carried signs that said "Equality for Everyone." They sang songs about freedom. They let the world know that segregation had to end.

A white judge ordered all the marches to stop. But King thought it was an unjust order. He decided to disobey the judge and continue the marches.

On April 12, 1963, police surrounded the marchers. Hundreds were grabbed and taken to jail. King was locked in a dark jail cell alone for a week.

King, shown here with Ralph Abernathy, was arrested on April 12, 1963, for disobeying a judge's order.

Birmingham police arrest a group of young marchers on May 2, 1963.

When King was released from jail, he and other civil rights leaders decided to try something new. On May 2, one thousand children marched downtown, singing and clapping. The Birmingham police carted them off to jail. The jails were overflowing.

The next day, more children marched. "We want freedom!" they shouted. This time the children were met by violence. Firefighters sprayed the children with their powerful hoses, knocking them down. The police ordered their dogs to attack the children. Finally, the police sent hundreds of children to jail.

King and his supporters were horrified by what had happened. That night on the television news, people all over the world saw what had happened to the children. More pictures appeared in the morning papers. Martin Luther King Jr. had the eyes of the world on Birmingham.

Television viewers were shocked by images showing violence toward peaceful protesters.

Finally, on May 7, the white Birmingham leaders met with King and other civil rights leaders. Together they made an agreement. Lunch counters, public bathrooms, drinking fountains, and department store fitting rooms would no longer be segregated. White businesses agreed to hire black people for decent jobs.

At last, the long struggle for "justice, freedom, and human dignity" was making a difference. King's movement of nonviolent resistance was working.

4 MARCHING FOR FREEDOM

King was showing the country that black people would stand up for their civil rights. He had awakened the nation. Black and white people all over the country began to speak out against hate and injustice. President John F. Kennedy wanted Congress to make a law ensuring civil rights for black Americans.

King and a group of other leaders decided to organize a march in Washington, D.C., to convince Congress to pass the bill. They hoped 100,000 people would come to Washington.

After months of planning, the march took place on August 28, 1963. King was amazed to see more than 200,000 people marching through Washington. Black people and white people walked together, arm in arm, from the Washington Monument to the Lincoln Memorial. They stood together on that hot day to listen to singers and speakers.

Thousands of civil rights marchers from all over the country made their way to hear King and others speak.

King delivers his "I Have a Dream" speech.

Martin Luther King was the last person to speak. In one of the most famous speeches ever, he talked about freedom, peace, and brotherhood. "I have a dream," he said, "that my four little children will one day live in a nation where they will not be judged by the color of their skin but by the content of their character. I have a dream today!" With his beautiful, strong words, Martin Luther King spread hope and understanding in Washington and all across the country.

King had become a major national leader. But he had many enemies. They hated King because of the rights he had won for black people. On November 22, 1963, President Kennedy was killed in Dallas, Texas. King didn't think he would have long to live either.

The new president, Lyndon B. Johnson, convinced Congress to pass the Civil Rights Act of 1964. The law says that African Americans cannot be treated unfairly. It protects a person's right to vote, find jobs, and use hotels, parks, restaurants, and other public places.

King looks on as President Johnson signs the Civil Rights Act of 1964.

An International Leader

In October 1964, King won the Nobel Peace Prize. The prize is awarded to a person from anywhere in the world who has done important work for peace and understanding. King was the youngest person ever to win. The prize included $54,000. Instead of keeping it for himself, King gave the money to the civil rights movement.

King was proud of this victory. But there was still so much to do. Laws in the United States said that black people had the right to vote. More often than not, officials in the South would not let black Americans use that right. King wanted to change that.

He went to Selma, Alabama, in January 1965 to help black people register to vote. For days, hundreds of African Americans marched to the courthouse. They stood in line for hours so they could register. Often they were told the office was closed. Many people, including King, were arrested. King's arrest made news around the world.

The white people of Selma did not want things to change. If blacks succeeded in voting, they would gain political power. As the registration continued, the police became violent. Many people were beaten.

Once again, King organized a march to protest injustice. On March 7, six hundred peaceful protesters began marching from Selma to Alabama's capital, Montgomery. The marchers tried to cross the Edmund Pettus Bridge, but white leaders ordered state troopers to beat them. The day became known as Bloody Sunday.

Troopers on horseback attacked these peaceful marchers in order to stop them from crossing the bridge.

After they came to the line of troopers on the bridge, the marchers knelt in prayer.

King was deeply upset. But he would not let white policemen stop black citizens from voting. Two days later, King led fifteen hundred people to the bridge. King was determined to cross it even though a judge had forbidden it. At the foot of the bridge, the peaceful marchers faced a solid line of troopers. It was too dangerous to go on. King stopped the march and led the protesters in prayer. Then he told them to turn around.

Later in March, the protesters successfully marched all the way across Pettus Bridge and on to Montgomery. Twenty thousand people joined them for a rally at the state capitol. There King told the group, "We will go on with the faith that nonviolence and its power transformed dark yesterdays into bright tomorrows."

Americans heard the message of King and the peaceful protesters. Soon after the protests in Selma, Congress passed the Voting Rights Act of 1965. The law would make sure that black people all over the United States would be able to vote.

5 THE DREAM GROWS

Martin Luther King Jr. had led African Americans in the South to many victories. In 1966, he decided to focus on northern cities such as Boston, New York, and Chicago. Those cities didn't have segregation laws. But African Americans there still faced discrimination and racism. King wanted to teach people how to use nonviolence to make changes in these cities.

King and Coretta (TOP CENTER WINDOW) greet visitors from their apartment in a Chicago slum.

King saw that white and black people lived in separate neighborhoods. Areas where black people lived were often poor and dirty. Landlords didn't take care of apartment buildings. The cities didn't always pick up garbage or fix streets.

King and his family moved to a poor neighborhood in Chicago. King worked to organize renters to improve their buildings. He led meetings about developing businesses run by black people.

But King found that many African Americans in the North could not be convinced to solve problems peacefully. People were tired of waiting for change.

King felt discouraged. So many people were so angry. But he did not give up. He kept looking for ways to make changes.

King believed blacks and whites needed to be united to solve problems. He had seen too much suffering caused by poverty for all people. He began planning a Poor People's March to Washington. He wanted to make Americans aware of the problems of poverty, as he had done with civil rights.

THE VIOLENT PATH

By the late 1960s, many black people had become angry and impatient. They thought King's nonviolent resistance moved too slowly. Some young black people wanted to use force to make changes. Violent riots broke out in Chicago, Detroit, Los Angeles, and other cities. Homes and businesses were burned. King knew it would take a long time to achieve equality. He didn't want to let violence stop his nonviolent movement.

In the spring of 1968, King went to Memphis, Tennessee, to work with a group of garbage collectors. They were among the poor people King wanted to help. He stayed at the Lorraine Motel near downtown Memphis.

On the night of April 3, King spoke to two thousand people. He told the people to keep working together for equal rights. He said, "I've been to the mountaintop. . . . and I've seen the promised land. I may not get there with you. But I want you to know tonight, that we, as a people, will get to the promised land."

That was Martin Luther King's last speech.

During his final speech, King talked about the progress that had been made toward freedom.

Mourners march behind King's coffin. King was buried in Atlanta, Georgia.

The following night, King stepped out on the balcony of his motel room. A loud bang rang out. King fell backward. He had been shot. He died within an hour.

The entire world was stunned by Martin Luther King's death. A march King had planned took place the next day. It turned into a memorial march of thirty thousand people. People everywhere had lost a powerful voice for peace and justice. But the gunman did not silence King's message. King's dream for equality lives on in people all over the world. People still find hope and inspiration in his powerful words.

TIMELINE

MARTIN LUTHER KING JR.
WAS BORN ON
JANUARY 15, 1929.

In the year . . .

1944   Martin entered Morehouse College in Atlanta.   Age 15

1948   he became a minister.
he began studying at Crozer Theological Seminary.

1951   he graduated from Crozer and went to Boston University.

1953   he married Coretta Scott.   Age 24

1954   he took a job as a minister in Montgomery, Alabama.

1955   his first daughter, Yolanda, was born.
the Montgomery bus boycott began.

1956   the Montgomery bus boycott ended when buses were desegregated.

1957   he formed the SCLC.
his son Martin Luther III was born.

1959   he and Coretta went to India.

1961   his son Dexter was born.

1963   his daughter Bernice was born.
he led protests against segregation in Birmingham, Alabama.
he gave his famous "I Have a Dream" speech in Washington, D.C.

1964   he won the Nobel Peace Prize.   Age 35

1965   he organized voting rights protests in Selma, Alabama.

1967   he began organizing a march to help poor people.

1968   he was shot and killed in Memphis, Tennessee.   Age 39

MARTIN LUTHER KING JR. DAY

After Martin Luther King Jr. died in 1968, many people wanted some way to show their respect for his memory. In 1983, the U.S. government created a holiday in his honor. Martin's birthday is January 15, so the nation celebrates his birthday on the third Monday of January every year. This special day is called Martin Luther King Jr. Day. Schools and many workplaces close. Cities across the country have marches, speeches, and other events to honor King. Celebrating Martin Luther King Jr. Day is an important way to remember King and what he worked for—peace, understanding, and equality.

FURTHER READING

NONFICTION

Fisher, Leonard Everett. *Gandhi.* **New York: Atheneum Books for Young Readers, 1995.** Tells the story of Gandhi's life and describes the way he worked for change without using violence. Illustrated with black and white paintings.

King, Martin Luther, Jr. *I Have a Dream.* **New York: Scholastic Press, 1997.** The text of Martin Luther King's famous "I Have a Dream" speech is illustrated with artwork by award-winning illustrators.

Weidt, Maryann N. *Rosa Parks.* **Minneapolis: Lerner Publications Company, 2003.** A biography of the woman whose refusal to give up her bus seat set off the Montgomery bus boycott.

Welch, Catherine A. *Children of the Civil Rights Era.* **Minneapolis: Carolrhoda Books, Inc., 2001.** Text and historical photographs illustrate the experiences of children who grew up during the civil rights movement of the 1950s and the 1960s.

FICTION

Davis, Ossie. *Just Like Martin.* **New York: Simon & Schuster Books for Young Readers, 1995.** In 1963, Alabama teenager Stone greatly admires Martin Luther King Jr. But he struggles with King's ideas as he faces violence at home and at church. For older readers.

WEBSITES

The King Center
<http://www.thekingcenter.org/> This organization was established by Coretta Scott King in 1968 in Atlanta. It runs

exhibits, a library, and King-related sites. Its website provides information about King's life, his ideas, and the center itself.

The Seattle Times: Martin Luther King Jr.
<http://seattletimes.nwsource.com/mlk/index.html> This site contains information about King and the civil rights movement. It offers a civil rights timeline, photos of King, recordings of King's speeches, information about Martin Luther King Jr. Day, and facts about King's life.

We Shall Overcome: Historic Places of the Civil Rights Movement
<http://www.cr.nps.gov/nr/travel/civilrights/index.htm> At this website, viewers can take a virtual tour of important places of the civil rights movement. Those places include the sites of marches and protests led by King, King's birthplace, and Dexter Avenue Baptist Church.

SELECT BIBLIOGRAPHY

Brinkley, Douglas. *Rosa Parks.* New York: A Lipper/Viking Book, 2000.

King, Martin Luther, Jr. *The Autobiography of Martin Luther King, Jr.* Edited by Clayborne Carson. New York: Warner Books, Inc., 1998.

Lewis, John, with Michael D'Orso. *Walking with the Wind: A Memoir of the Movement.* New York: Harcourt Brace & Company, 1998.

Schulke, Flip, and Penelope McPhee. *King Remembered.* New York: Pocket Books, 1986.

Siebold, Thomas, ed. *Martin Luther King Jr.* San Diego: Greenhaven Press, Inc., 2000.

INDEX

Acknowledgments

For photographs: Independent Photo Service, p. 4; Schomburg Center for Research in Black Culture, pp. 7, 17, 20; Library of Congress, pp. 8, 18; National Archives, photo no. 16–N–6435, p. 9, photo no. 306–PS–62–6446, p. 26; Everett Collection, pp. 10, 12; © Flip Schulke/CORBIS, pp. 13, 36, 37; AP/Wide World Photos, pp. 19, 22, 27; © Bettmann/CORBIS, pp. 21, 28, 29, 33, 40, 42; *The Tennessean,* p. 25; NBC Photo, p. 32; Lyndon B. Johnson Library (276–10–64), p. 34; Hulton/Archive, p. 43; Carol Simowitz, p. 45. Front cover, Flip Schulke/CORBIS. Back cover, © Bettmann/CORBIS.
For quoted material: pp. 8, 30, 33, 38, 42, Martin Luther King Jr., *The Autobiography of Martin Luther King, Jr.,* Clayborne Carson, ed., (New York: Warner Books, Inc., 1998); p. 19, Flip Schulke and Penelope McPhee, *King Remembered* (New York: Pocket Books, a division of Simon & Schuster, 1986).